YOUR CAT WON'T DO THAT!

Observations and Advice for Cat Companions
from a Longtime Cat-Sitter

Stephen Taylor

D1739010

Print ISBN: 978-1-64719-750-6
Ebook ISBN: 978-1-64719-751-3

Published by BookLocker.com, Inc., St. Petersburg, Florida.

Printed on acid-free paper.

This publication contains the opinions and ideas of its author. It is intended to provide helpful and informative material on the subjects addressed in the publication. It is sold with the understanding that the author and publisher are not engaged in rendering medical, health, or any other kind of personal professional services in the book. The reader should consult his or her medical, health, veterinary, or other competent professional before adopting any of the suggestions in this book or drawing inferences from it.

The author and publisher specifically disclaim all responsibility for any liability, loss, or risk, personal or otherwise, which is incurred as a consequence, directly or indirectly, of the use and application of any of the contents of this book.

BookLocker.com, Inc.
2021

First Edition

Library of Congress Cataloguing in Publication Data
Taylor, Stephen
Your Cat Won't Do That! by Stephen Taylor
Library of Congress Control Number: 2021915126

Dedication

To my family's cats, W.T., Gus, and especially my dear, departed Maxi...to my long-standing clients, departed and living: Callie and Louise; Buster and Tyler; Buddy and Whiskey; Puffin and Audie; Willow and Lulu...and to all cats and their loving companions everywhere.

Table of Contents

Introduction

It happened every time I took on a new cat-sitting client[1]. In addition to hearing all the usual generalizations about watching someone's cat—where the food was kept, where the litter box was located, how long Kitty and I would be sharing quarters with each other—I inevitably heard a list of particulars describing what the cat was expected do while I was there:

"Tigger will come in and sit on your lap whenever you're watching TV."

"Don't leave any clothes lying around on the floor—Garfield will pee on them."

"Be careful going in and out—Felix will follow you out if you're not careful."

"Tom loves playing with your shoelaces."

"Scratchy likes to cuddle up on the bed by your head when you go to sleep at night."

---

[1] Please note: I think of the cats I sat with as my clients just as much as I did the people who hired me. When I mention a "client" or "clients" in this book, sometimes I'm talking about the human companion, sometimes I'm talking about the cat, sometimes both.

Throughout my decade of professional cat-sitting, in many homes housing numerous cats, I heard these and similar claims, some several times over. The cat companions who passed along these nuggets of information—really, misinformation—meant well. And, in a very few cases, those observations turned out to be true.

But most of the time these tips turned out to be wrong—so much so that I developed a general rule for all such advice from cat companions: whatever

Exhibit A: a Cat who Won't Do That!

you tell me to expect Kitty to do while you're gone...
Your Cat Won't Do That!

What's up with that?

This brief book is my attempt to bridge the gap between what cat companions tell the cat-sitter about their feline friends, and what they *should* be saying about them.

In addition to covering that main topic, I will also offer helpful hints about how you should approach having a sitter take care of your cat. This includes advice on feeding; on the litter box (both the box itself and what goes in it); a sitter's thoughts on the 'indoor vs. outdoor' conundrum; the particulars of multi-cat households; and words on other items of interest.

Cats by their nature are very particular about their living arrangements. Every time a cat's trusted humans go away and leave her[2] under a

---

2 Throughout this book, whenever I refer to a client cat, I will generally use 'she' or 'her,' unless I'm talking about a specific male cat. This is mainly because the majority of my cat clients have been female; it should not be read as a preference for female cats. Conversely, I will usually refer to 'your sitter' as 'he' or 'him' using myself as the model.

stranger's care, it can be a stressful and frustrating experience for the cat—and, for that matter, for the stranger, too.

Does it really matter if you tell your cat-sitter that Kitty will curl up next to him on the couch while he's watching TV, and instead she curls up on the back of the couch behind the sitter? Probably not.

Does it matter if you tell the sitter that Kitty likes to lay down in the office in the afternoon to catch the sun's rays, and instead she doesn't leave the bedroom for two days? Yes, that does matter. Almost certainly, it matters a great deal.

What's the difference? That's what this book is all about.

We'll start with what your cat will do when the sitter is with her, and what she won't do—and all the ways in which that difference can be very, very important.

An important note: As I say, I was a longtime cat-sitter, having spent a decade (2009-2018) taking care of a small stable of regular clients. I also served many years as a volunteer "cat care partner" at a local animal shelter, where I spent countless hours socializing with hundreds of cats. And, for over thirty years, my family has had several much-loved feline members. That means I've spent a lot of time around cats, and I've learned a lot about taking care of them. But—and I need to emphasize this—*I'm not a veterinarian.* Anything I say in this book that sounds like cat health advice should be taken as an amateur's opinion. Always be sure to follow up with your cat's vet on any question this book raises regarding your own cat's health. Even if your cat "won't do that"—or anything else you tell her to do—please take every precaution to keep your Kitty healthy.

Now that we have that detail out of the way, let's move on to what your cat will and won't do—and why your sitter needs to know all about that!

Chapter 1:
Your Cat Won't Do That!

You've made your vacation plans. You've booked the flight, the hotel, and the rental car. You've planned your itinerary down to the most minute details. Everything is taken care of. You've even found a reliable cat-sitter, one who comes highly recommended by your good friend. You meet the sitter and go over all the details. You tell him about every habit your furry friend has. Hopefully, you've covered everything your sitter will need to know to make sure your cat has as good a time while you're gone as you will.[3]

As likely as not, however, your report on your cat's habits will be of little use to your cat-sitter. Generally speaking, whatever you've told him about how he can expect Kitty to behave, your cat won't do that!

---

[3] You should always give your sitter a list of vital information regarding your cat, especially on a first visit. Providing a kitty checklist—or even a "book" on your cat—always makes everything go smoother for everyone involved.

Expectations vs. Reality

Your instinct to tell your cat-sitter what your cat does is not wrong; information about your cat's behavior will be vital for your cat-sitter. After all, a sitter's primary focus is always one simple matter: Is the cat I'm watching OK?

By OK, I mean: Is the cat safe? Healthy? Happy? Those are your cat-sitter's goals.

How is all that determined? Largely by behavior. The major gauges of a cat's well-being are all behavior related: eating (or not); using the litter box regularly (or not); and what she is doing with the rest of her time. Since cats may be the world's most inscrutable animals, such telltale behavioral signals are the only reliable way to judge whether or not a cat is healthy and happy.

Because your sitter will have little or no experience with your particular cat's normal behavior—especially on a first visit—he will only have what you tell him to serve as a guide to what is normal for your cat. Thus, it's important for your sitter to know just what are your cat's normal behaviors.

That's where the problem arises. What, in fact, are your cat's "normal" behaviors? All of those tics and traits that you mentioned to the sitter before you left are going to be her normal behaviors... when you're at home. But those behaviors— particularly the ones that directly involve you—are not really all that useful for your sitter. After all, you're not going to be there—that's why you hired a cat-sitter!

When you are not at home, your cat is unlikely to follow most—or perhaps even *any*—of those habits that specifically relate to you. So all of those little things that your cat does that directly involve you, while they may be fun and enjoyable to relate, are not exactly useful information for your sitter.

Independent Normal Behaviors

This raises the obvious question: If your sitter doesn't need to know how your cat behaves when you're at home, then what can you tell the sitter about your cat's normal behavior?

This may seem like an unsolvable conundrum. You may ask, "How can I tell you what my cat does when I'm not around? I'm not around to see it!" However, the answer is, if you think about it, actually easy and obvious: tell the sitter the kinds of things your cat does when you are around but that don't involve you. In other words, what are your cat's normal behaviors that are *independent* of you? Those are the important baseline behaviors that establish what your kitty does when all is well and she is feeling good.

A good way to figure out what those behaviors are is to keep in mind what you discover your cat doing when you come home from being out for a while. Where is she? What part of the house is she in? Is she sleeping? Has she left signs of playing while you were gone? Such signs can include scattered toys, misplaced (or even broken) objects, maybe a roll of toilet paper that's torn and unwound.

Those kinds of behaviors may seem insignificant, or may even be small or large annoyances, but if such actions are something your cat does regularly—without any evidence of some underlying problem—they can be important signals that, according to your cat, all is well.

On the Lookout for Anything Unusual

Remember, the way to tell if something is wrong with your cat is if she is acting out of the ordinary. Your sitter will always be on the lookout for the primary indicators of your cat's health and well-being: eating habits and litter box usage. Any persistent deviation in those habits will send up a red flag about your cat.

Beyond those basics, however, a more thorough knowledge of your cat's particular behaviors can be invaluable. If Kitty has a habit of pulling the towels off the racks in the bathroom, and your vet has found nothing wrong with her health-wise, then that's a good thing for your cat-sitter to know. If the cat keeps it up, even when some unfamiliar human is occupying her space, then that probably shows that your cat has come to terms with this temporary change in the scheme and concluded that it's acceptable.

Conversely, if you have never observed your cat to spend any time in that back bedroom, be sure to mention that to your sitter as well. That way, if the sitter finds Kitty curled up on the bed in there, especially if she's not doing anything else for long periods of time, that's a pretty good sign that something is wrong.

Having a baseline knowledge of your cat's normal, independent behaviors can be crucial when it comes to a sitter's chief duty: making sure your cat remains healthy while you're away. If Kitty starts deviating from her usual independent behaviors, that can be an important signal that something significant is wrong with your cat—a problem that goes beyond basic peevishness over

If a nap in the laundry basket is normal, then your cat is saying, "It's all good here!"

the fact that you had the poor taste to leave your beloved cat with this weird stranger.

If the deviation is a one-off act—a one-time protest against the change in the routine—your sitter can probably relax and assume that you cat is, if not happy, then healthy at the very least. But if such abnormal behaviors persist, that may indicate that a vet visit is in order. Your sitter's ability to make that judgment can be the difference between a good or a very bad outcome to your trip, for everyone involved.

In sum, when you're giving your cat-sitter— particularly a new sitter, though even an old friend can use refresher now and then—a lowdown on your cat's behaviors, try to focus on the things Kitty does that don't directly involve any members of the regular household. A cat who follows a routine of basic, independent behaviors is a cat who is healthy and happy—exactly the way your sitter wants her to remain.

Of course, the most fundamental cat behavior involves eating. In the next chapter, we'll go over a few feeding-related matters—things that can ensure that your cat gets along well with her new friend, the cat-sitter.

Chapter 2:
Not by Bread—or Tuna—Alone: Feeding the Cat

Feeding the cat is the most basic, fundamental, and essential part of a cat-sitter's job. While you're gone, your cat can do without your company; can live without a playmate; can probably even get by without a litter box (though I wouldn't recommend that, for sure). But without food, your cat is a goner.

So feeding the cat is important, not just for you and your kitty in your day-in, day-out life, but also for your cat and her sitter, too.

Feeding the cat seems like it should be pretty straightforward, and for the most part, it is. Get some food, make it accessible for Kitty, and away she goes. But there a few considerations to keep in mind, especially where your cat-sitter is concerned.

Making the Bond

Giving a cat its food is the primary way in which we humans form bonds with our feline friends. Your cat accepts you as her friend and family in large part because you are the source of the food she needs and craves. Instead of having to scratch and claw her way to a meal out there in the alley, her food gets set out for her by you, all yummy and effortless. No wonder your cat loves you! Food is a great bond-maker.

That same dynamic can work for your cat and her sitter, too. In fact, dishing out the vittles is the best way a cat-sitter can get a new client to trust him. You get on a cat's good side in a hurry, even if you're a relative stranger, if you're laying down that dish of "Gravy-Lover's Grilled Tuna." Given that fact, here are a few things to think about when it comes to feeding your cat, not just when the sitter's watching your furry friend, but when you're home with her, too.

Active vs. Passive

Depending upon which type of food you give your cat—dry vs. canned—serving duties can run the gamut from easy to practically nonexistent.

Automatic feeders make feeding your cat a breeze. You don't have to make any real effort to dish out the food—the cat or the mechanism will make the effort for you. Just fill up the hopper every few days and it's all taken care of. That can be a real timesaver on a day-to-day basis. The ability to let your cat feed herself through the use of an automatic feeder is a big reason why cats have a reputation for being such "low maintenance" pets.

Of course, when it's a cat-sitter who's in charge of dishing out the food, an automatic feeder provides a big insurance policy against a sitter who doesn't come through for your cat, for whatever reason. Kitty won't go hungry, even if you happen to get a cat-sitter who turns out to be downright negligent.

*Whiskey enjoys a meal from the automatic feeder,
the cat-sitter's best frenemy.*

But there's an important component to feeding a cat that auto-feeders eliminate: feeding as a social act, as a venue for bonding. Just as you make your bond with your cat by feeding her, so too will your cat-sitter. Nothing helps build a positive relationship between your cat and this new person who has entered her life than feeding time. When your sitter places a bowl of yummy food in front of Kitty, that act tells her, "You can trust this stranger. This person is your friend."

During my career as a cat-sitter, I spent time both in homes where the cats were fed by hand each day, and in homes where the cats took their meals from automatic feeders. There's nothing wrong with giving a cat its food through a feeder; it's fine to let your cat take her meals out of a hopper rather than from someone's hand. I don't think most cats really mind getting their grub from an auto-feeder. Nor, from what I've seen, is there a particular health issue with just giving your cat dry food. (Obviously, most commercially available auto-feeders are for dishing out kibble; maybe someone out there can make millions developing an auto-delivery system that opens cans of moist food and plops it into a waiting bowl.) In short, I believe auto-feeding is OK, and I wouldn't say cats who are only fed that way are suffering in any way.

But I will say this: between my clients' homes where the cat was fed by a hopper, and the homes where I did the feeding by dishing out the meal myself, my cat clients and I formed the tightest bonds where I did the dishing out. Having the opportunity to establish that day-to-day rhythm of calling the cat to the kitchen, listening to her "sing for her supper," talking to her as she eagerly anticipated her food, and then being able to hand down that dish—and be personally associated with the yummies being served—was a crucial component in getting someone else's cat to accept me as part of her life. Everything else that grew from that forged bond—our playtimes together; our cuddling sessions; the cat's willingness to accept me as a routine part of her life, and thus behave well for me—gave my clients an experience that was both richer and more normal while their family members were away. And that, after all, is what you're trying to achieve when you ask a sitter to come into your home and take care of your feline friends.

So while it's not a problem to feed your cat using an automatic dispenser, I strongly recommend that you work some kind of direct feeding into your cat care routine. That will give your sitter the opportunity to enjoy the bond-making benefits of serving the cat's supper.

Fantastic Plastic

Here's an odd little personal preference of my own: I recommend that clients keep at least one or two plastic forks for feeding the cat her canned food.

Why? I find that plastic forks—particularly the ones that have ridges behind the tines—seem to work better at mashing up canned cat food than metal utensils do. Something about their flexibility makes them good for that use. I have no evidence that cats like their wet food mashed up into a finer paste. I've always just assumed it to be true, and my experience seems to bear that out. A finer chop seems to get more thoroughly eaten, and plastic forks provide that nicely-mashed consistency.

Quite apart from their utility, plastic forks also reduce the "Yuck!" factor. Few of us want eat our own food with the same fork that was used to mash up fish guts, regardless of how often it has been washed. You can't always tell by looking at a fork how clean it is. A little utensil separation goes a long way.

So please, if at all possible, save those take-out forks for feline food preparation.

The Can or The Bag?

Even if you decide to avoid the auto-feeder, you will still be left with the choice of whether to give your cat dry food, or moist food, or—and this is most common—some combination of the two. For your cat-sitter, each has its advantages and disadvantages.

Dry food's biggest benefit is convenience. It can be dished out quickly, easily, and without making a mess; that's something to consider if your sitter is someone (I will confess, like me) who is not necessarily the tidiest individual. If your sitter keeps odd hours—for instance, I'm a nighthawk, while two of my best human clients were early risers—dry food can be a boon for both the sitter and the cat. It can be left out for Kitty to take her meal at her leisure without spoiling. And, as it is usually bought in bulk, you can stock up a ready supply of kibble that will last for your sitter's entire stay, even if you will be gone for an extended period. For convenience, dry food can't be beat.

Moist food, on the other hand, comes with its own advantages. Most cats seem to like it better than dry food. That may be because with canned food you can serve a different flavor from day to day, whereas kibble tends to be bought in big bags and thus is the same bowl after bowl after bowl. Variety is, after all, the spice of nine lives. There's also the visceral pleasure that comes from that sharp sound of a pull-top can being opened; it's about the best "dinner bell" around, and that crisp, metallic rasp tends to bring cats running. That supports the social aspect of mealtime mentioned above; opening a can of moist food literally sends a signal to your cat that it's time to pay attention to the human in her home.

Ideally, a combination of both dry and moist food should be in your cat's diet. Serving both kibble and wet food covers all the bases of convenience and sitter/cat bonding. The majority of my clients had me feed their cats just such a combination, and that menu always worked quite well both for me and the cats I watched. If you're a cat companion who sticks to one kind of food and not the other, I would suggest you reconsider and see if a combo of the two types of food will work for you and your cat.

Perhaps you feed your cat one type of food or the other exclusively because your veterinarian recommends that you do so. I'm not a vet, so I can't say one way or the other which type of food is healthier. If you have a recommendation, I suggest you follow it, and let your sitter adapt to what your cat needs.

There is one note of caution I can sound from personal experience when it comes to cat health and the choice between dry food and moist meals. If you have a cat who is overweight, you might want to limit or even eliminate the dry food. The convenience of the kibble can work against those cats who are prone to gaining extra pounds. Because dry food is usually left sitting there in its bowl or feeder, it is always available to be eaten—and thus can be eaten in excess. Controlling your cat's portions via cans of moist food can be easier, simply because it's less likely to be left out like an all-day buffet.

Of course, you may be really, really concerned about your cat's health through her diet. Perhaps you will choose the third option: preparing your cat's food from scratch. Some cat companions do this, buying particular cuts of meat from the butcher's shop and serving portions of "real" food to their furry family members.

As a sitter, I have no experience with that sort of feeding; all of my clients stuck to commercially prepared cat food, in one form or another, so there's little I can say about scratch-prepared meals. If you do scratch-feed your cat, and if you're going to get a sitter to watch her, be sure to go over your preferred food prep practices carefully and comprehensively with the sitter before you leave. Show him everything from start to finish, because as likely as not, your sitter will not have any experience feeding a cat anything other than store-bought cat food. The last thing you want is an inexperienced person giving your cat a meal with small bones in it, or any other (literal) recipes for disaster.

As you know, what goes in eventually must come out. That fact remains true even when you're not home. All that food will ultimately find its way into the litter box, and that's where we're headed next—where I'll share with you some of a cat-sitter's biggest pet peeves.

Chapter 3:
Let's Talk Litter

Cleaning the litter box is probably the biggest job the cat-sitter has when he is in your home. Feeding is arguably more important—after all, it keeps your cat healthy and alive—but many feline-friendly families give their kitties only dry food, and use automatic feeders to dish out the edibles. In that case, the amount of kitchen effort required of your cat-sitter may be minimal.

Not so when it comes to the litter box. Even cats who get generous amounts of outdoor time will still come inside to use their litter boxes. In a house that has more than one cat, scooping the box is an everyday task, and—depending upon how "productive" those cats are—it can be a major chore.

The job is often made more onerous by certain mistakes made by cat companions when setting up their kitties' privies. Let's take a look at some of those mistakes, and how they can be avoided, to make for a better box experience—certainly for the sitter, and hopefully for you and your cat, too.

The Litter Box

Most of the mistakes cat companions make when setting up their cats' bathrooms have to do with the box itself. The dimensions, shape, and features of the litter box can all contribute to making each day's "shake and scoop" into either a quick, breezy task, or an arduous chore. Common mistakes include:

Too big. People have a tendency to give their cats a litter box that's way too big. This is especially true in households that have more than one cat. As should be obvious, a box that is gigantic can be problematic to clean well. Overlarge boxes can be difficult to pick up and shake to reveal your cat's waste (a process I like to call "panning for brown gold").

This is especially true because a large box encourages a related mistake: filling the box with too much litter. Too much litter makes a box too heavy to properly sift for disposables. It can become something like going to the playground and trying to pick up the kids' sandbox: only a giant could actually accomplish the task.

Even if you just leave the box on the floor and rake through the sand for those lumps, too much square footage creates problems. Not only does it require more effort, but having to plow through something like an acre of sand to find those "buried treasures" will almost guarantee that some of the waste will be missed—and that's not good for both the sitter and your cat. For the sitter, an unclean box is simply frustrating; for your cat, it can be downright unhealthy.

The best policy: keep your cat's box compact. If you think one small box is not enough territory for multiple cats, get another small box. I'd rather clean two or three small boxes than one or two large ones, every day of the week.

Bad placement. If you follow the above rule and get a small box, it should be much easier to follow this second rule: place your cat's box in an area that's accessible and relatively open. There's a temptation to place the litter box in a tucked away, out of sight (and smell) location in a far corner of the house. Obviously, you don't want the litter box in some high-traffic part of your home, but please don't place the box in a spot that's difficult to reach, either.

A Scoop for Every Box

If your house has more than one litter box, do yourself a favor and get a separate scoop for each box. It may seem like a very small difference to equip each box with its own scoop versus carrying one scoop between multiple boxes, but setting up each box with its own scoop makes a relatively easy task that much easier. This is especially true if there's a second or third box on a different floor from the main box. Since we tend to spend most of our time on one floor of a house, that upstairs or downstairs box can get overlooked. If there's a scoop with that isolated box, your sitter (or you, for that matter) is much more likely to clean it out in the odd moments when he is passing by. So if you don't already have one, I recommend getting that extra scoop for each box.

For instance, don't wedge the box into a corner next to a refrigerator or washing machine or some such large, heavy appliance that will not budge. In other words, don't situate the pan next to anything that leaves no room to move it around. A back corner of a closet isn't ideal either, especially since closets tend to fill up until there's no free space left. The litter box will almost certainly wind up crammed in there without any maneuvering room. There needs to be some wiggle room around the box in order to properly lift, sift, and scoop. Make sure you place Kitty's commode in a relatively commodious space for easy access.

Lastly, if there's a lid on your cat's box—these days, most boxes come with lids—there needs to be some open space nearby where the lid can be set aside during the scooping process. And please be sure not to pile any objects atop the lid.

The bottom line: keep the box in a relatively open and accessible space.

The wrong shape. Here's a major tip that will make not just your sitter's task easier, but your own life easier, too.

Almost all litter boxes these days are rectangular, with varying degrees of rounded corners. Think about all the times you've scooped your cat's litter and had to dig one of those urine-sand-clay clumps out of one of those corners. Sometimes you'll get a clump that adheres so tightly to the corner that no amount of shaking the pan, thumping the sides of the box, or smacking the box against the floor will dislodge it. Why does this happen? Because the corner provides the clump with two surfaces to cling to. It's like a perfect litter-clump trap.

Cats seem to have a perverse preference for dropping their pee right where it will be the most difficult to scoop out of the box. I can't tell you how many times I've had to excavate a clump out of an inconvenient corner. This often results in a clump that breaks apart and scatters crumbles into the rest of the sand. Yuck! Such excavations require more effort and produce a litter box that's not cleaner, but actually dirtier, than when you began.

Ideally, the whole box should be round. If you have a circular litter box, there are no corners in which the clumps can stick. My Maxi had a small, round box for years, and her litter was usually a breeze to clean. A couple of quick shakes will pull the clumps away from the box's wall. If you do need to help things along with the scoop, the round sides make it easy to scrape the clumps away from the wall. The lack of heavy digging and scraping keeps the clumps intact, so the rest of the litter stays clean.

Our household's litter box: small, round, latchless, lightweight... perfect!

Do yourself a favor: get your cat a round litter box, or (if you can't find a perfectly round pan) a rectangular box with well-rounded corners. You and your sitter will be happier for it.

A bad lid. As noted above, most boxes today come with a lid. This is good for your cat's privacy, and presumably for holding in the box's most noxious smells—but it can also provide an extra annoyance when you, or your sitter, has to clean the box.

My single biggest peeve with litter box lids is with the ones that come with latches. Somebody please explain it to me: why, oh why, do these lids have latches? At our house we have a litter box that has a lid without latches, one that simply rests on the rim of the pan, and never once has it spontaneously leapt off its seat and tumbled away from the box. What possible reason could there be for securing the litter box's lid to the pan with latches? Does anyone really expect their cat to suddenly "hulk out" and burst upward out of her box? Seriously, I've never found one benefit to having latches on the litter box lid.

Conversely, I've always found those latches to be a major annoyance. Loosening them adds one extra step to the task of cleaning the litter box. Sometimes the latches are balky and put up a fight when you're trying to loosen them. Then, when the cleaning is finished, the latches make re-placing the lid another annoyance. They often get in the way of seating the lid properly on the edge of the pan.

It's a small thing, to be sure, but it's a frustrating thing, especially because those latches are so unnecessary. As with all things, make life easier, not harder: buy a box with a latchless lid. And if you already have a box that has those latches, go ahead and remove them.

The Litter

There are a couple of mistakes my clients—and probably every other cat companion—makes with regards to litter.

Too much litter. There seems to be a common misperception among cat companions that their cats need huge, Sahara Desert-like expanses of sand in order to be happy using their litter boxes. This relates to the problem of overly large litter boxes described above. It probably also arises from people buying litter in huge, oversized jugs or feed-store-sized bags. But even those who use relatively small boxes tend to fill those pans with way too much litter. It's excessive and unnecessary, and it makes the task of scooping the pan more difficult.

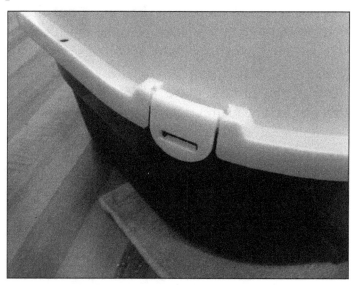

A litter box lid with latches: Bad Human!

Too much litter makes it impossible to completely scoop out the bad stuff from the box; there's too much material in which the little crusty pieces of turd and urine-clumps can hide for a scooping to get everything out of there. An incomplete cleaning is not just a nuisance for your sitter. Those dirty little grains may be small enough to pass our notice, but your cat has finer senses, and she may very well make a point of noticing the box's lack of perfect cleanliness. Cats are creatures who are always on the lookout for excuses to be, shall we say, problematic. If Kitty is not pleased by the condition of her litter, she may resort to troubling behaviors like going outside the box as a form of protest. Thus, overfilling the box may wind up being a self-defeating tactic. Avoid it if at all possible.

How much litter should go in the box? At the shelter where I was a volunteer, the rule of thumb for the proper amount of sand for an average-sized litter box—roughly 18 inches long by 15 inches wide—was half a ten-pound bag of material, or five pounds of litter. Note that that's five pounds going into an *empty* box; the boxes at the shelter got filled after having been washed and dried. A small box—generally, a half-sized box used only for kittens or in cages in the quarantine areas—got half that amount, or a quarter of a ten-pound bag.

That's it. For most standard, adult-sized boxes, just five pounds of sand will do. I suggest buying a ten-pound bag of your brand (if you can get that size; otherwise, you might need to do a bit of tricky math), pouring half of it into your cat's (cleaned and emptied) litter box, and carefully noting just how much that amount fills the box. Five pounds of sand is really not that much—generally, it's about enough to cover the bottom of a standard pan to about 1 to 1-1/2 inches deep. Anything else is excessive, unnecessary, and makes the task of scooping out the box more difficult than it needs to be. So go easy on the litter, please.

Also, please note: completely emptying and cleaning your litter boxes once in a while is a good idea. It's easy to fall into the habit of continually pouring fresh sand in on top of old litter—I'm guilty of that myself sometimes—but that's not an ideal practice. For maximum cleanliness and odor control, dump everything out of the box on a regular schedule.

If you want your sitter to perform a full dump and fresh fill while you are gone, you should explicitly spell that duty out with him before you leave—but try not to make the task too arduous with an overfilled box. If you leave an overfilled box for your sitter, that will make the task more troublesome and less likely to be done. He may just stick to regular scooping and leave the full dump for you to take care of when you get home.

The wrong litter. During my years as a cat-sitter, I encountered just about every brand of litter in my clients' homes, and one thing became clear to me: most of what's out there on the market is not very good. Some brands are stickier than others (exacerbating the corner-clump problem described above). Some brands hardly clump at all, with the clumps falling apart at the slightest touch and polluting the rest of the litter. Some brands, despite their promises, do little to control odor, while others are so dusty that one session of scooping the box will leave you feeling like you just ended a shift in a coal mine.

What litter works best? Personally, I've always liked the stuff you get by scooping it out yourself from the big bin in the back of the large chain store's cat supply section. It clumps well, rarely

---

The Glasses Test

Here's a tip for judging whether or not you're using good litter, one that glasses-wearing cat companions may already have learned for themselves.

When you go to clean your cat's litter, do so wearing glasses, either your prescription lenses or (if you're blessed with good eyesight) a pair of sunglasses. Perform your "shake and scoop" as usual; when you're done, remove the glasses and take a good look at the lenses. Are they suddenly covered with dust? If so, that's a pretty good indication that your cat's litter is too dusty. You might want to try a different brand and see if you can get better, cleaner results.

Just be sure your cat agrees to make the change. If Kitty will only use that dusty litter…you may be stuck with it, and it may be time to buy a special pair of "shake and scoop" goggles.

---

sticks to the walls of the box, does a decent job at odor control, and isn't overly dusty. As an added bonus, it's relatively inexpensive, particularly if you bring back your jug and scoop up a refill. And, perhaps best of all, my cats have always seemed to like using it—never a small consideration when you're talking about creatures as finicky as cats!

Now, as they say, "your mileage may vary" when it comes to your choice of litter. Your preference—and your cat's preference—may not lean towards the store brand described above. That's fine, but whatever litter you get, I do advise that you judge your choice based on the criteria listed above: clumping, stickiness, dustiness, and odor control. Get the right combination of good performance in those areas, and you, your cat, and your cat-sitter, will all be happy.

The last word: whenever you're in any doubt about your cat's litter box, go to your local animal shelter—almost all decent-sized metro areas have at least one well-run charitable shelter these days—and see what they do about litter for their adoptable cats. After all, those folks are the experts at taking care of cats; they get plenty of practice.

Just copy what the shelter staff do, and your cat should be all set. Just remember that your sitter needs to deal with that box, too!

So far, we've looked at the two most basic aspects of cat-sitting: feeding and litter. Both are fundamental to keeping your cat healthy. Sometimes, however, your sitter may need to go beyond health basics with your cat. In the next chapter, we'll discuss some important considerations for when your cat needs a little extra care.

Chapter 4:
If You Don't Have Your Health…

Do I even need to mention that it's important to make sure that your cat is healthy *before* you leave her with a sitter? Apparently, I do. I once had a client set up a stay with me only to inform me—as the family was headed out the door—that one of their cats had worms. I've had the harrowing experience of having to administer daily fluid injections to a dying cat. I've also had lots of experience giving cats oral medicines, a situation that can range from a relatively easy transaction to an all-out cat-vs.-sitter war. Truly, as with people, if a cat doesn't have her health, it's a big deal—for both the cat and the sitter.

Sitter vs. Vet
It's good to start off by reminding everyone that, in almost every case, your cat-sitter is not a veterinarian. (As noted in the disclaimer in the introduction, I'm not a vet—just a longtime cat companion and sitter.) Obviously, anyone who

chooses to perform cat-sitting duties, either as a volunteer or professionally, probably loves cats and has had cats in his or her life. That's helpful, but it still doesn't mean your cat-sitter is trained and certified to provide care for a sick or injured animal. Any ailments that arise while you are gone will mean a trip to the vet's office—and that can mean anything from another minor expense for you to something much more serious for everyone involved.

Sometimes you'll get lucky and find a sitter who works for a vet; some veterinary assistants will perform sitting duties for favorite patients. Chances are good that such a person will have experience dealing with cats in various degrees of distress, and that will help if a trip to the vet's office becomes necessary. However, even in that case, that veterinary staffer-turned-sitter may not necessarily know everything there is to know about treating a sick cat.

The above also applies if your sitter is someone who volunteers with cats at the local shelter. (Again, I was one of that breed.) That person will be familiar with cats, but ultimately may not have any more knowledge about treating an unhealthy cat than you or any other cat companion.

Whatever your sitter's background, if your cat gets sick or injured, your sitter will have no choice but to take your cat to the vet. That will not be a lot of fun for anyone. If you think cats are unwilling to cooperate under normal circumstances, wait until a relative stranger tries to pack one who is sick or hurt into a carrier. Nevertheless, nothing good will happen for your sick or injured cat without a visit to the doctor. Whether your cat is the cooperative sort or a combat veteran, your sitter must err on the side of caution and take your cat to the vet if he thinks Kitty is having a serious problem. After all, the last thing a responsible sitter wants to do is ignore a potential problem and wind up with a dead cat on his hands!

The bottom line should be obvious: make sure your cat is healthy before you leave home. If possible, schedule your cat's next routine checkup for a week or two before you are slated to leave. You'll save everyone a lot of anguish down the line if you do. If it turns out that your cat is sick, and you can do so, stay home. Your trip may be, in your eyes, the opportunity of a lifetime, but you have to weigh that against your cat's one and only lifetime. The "nine lives" thing is a myth; cats only get one shot at life, just like us. If illness has your cat's life in the balance, do you really want to possibly miss out on your last precious moments with your beloved Kitty? That, too, is a once-in-a-lifetime experience; you won't get a second chance to say goodbye.

If you must go away despite your cat's ailment, consider boarding her at your vet's office. Many veterinary practices offer boarding, and leaving your cat with a professional who knows her medical history is the best way to ensure that a sick Kitty gets the best care possible while you're gone.

Basic Cat Care

All of the above notwithstanding, there are some health-related duties that any worthwhile cat-sitter should be able to accomplish.

Chief among these tasks is giving your cat medicine. Most professional sitters will include administering medicine as part of their normal services, though some may charge extra for difficult tasks such as giving a reluctant cat an oral medicine or shots. Be sure to ask, as part of the process of setting up your sitter's stay, whether or not he charges extra for such duties. Always ask your sitter if he has given a cat any medicines before; *never* assume that a cat-sitter has experience with administering medicine to a cat.

Whether there's an extra charge or not, be sure to go over with your sitter any dosing information for your cat.

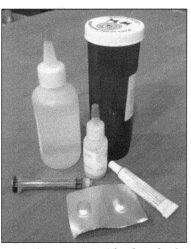

If Kitty gets a drop or two of an oral medication mixed in with her food, that's not a big deal. In that case, you can just leave instructions and make sure there's an ample supply of the medicine to cover

Dosing any cat with a bunch of medicines can be a very tricky task. If your Kitty needs her meds, make sure your sitter is up to the task before you go away.

the period while you're away. If you will be away for an extended time, make sure there's refill information on file with your cat's vet and/or pharmacy.

If your cat's medication needs to be directly administered—whether via pills, or a liquid mixture delivered orally via dropper, or even shots—then it is absolutely essential that you set up a time when your sitter can come over to your home and get an in-person primer on giving your cat her meds. Every cat has his or her own reaction to being given medicine; the vast majority of them hate it. So it's important that your sitter gets a chance to go over the procedure while you are still at home and able to oversee the process in detail.

It's always best to make sure that your sitter is able to administer medicine before you leave. I speak from experience. In my career, I had as many failed attempts to dose a cat as successes. It's a task that I still struggle with, even when dealing with my own cats.

For example, early in my cat-sitting career, I had one client, Callie, who needed to take an oral medicine. Due to my lack of expertise, I was unable to get a full dose of the mixture into her, no matter how much effort I put into it. Callie fought and squirmed and refused to swallow her medicine. When I got some part of the dose in her mouth, she resorted to letting the medicine drool out through her lips, even when I held her head still and stroked her neck (the standard procedure for getting a cat to swallow). It's very distressing when you can't get a cat to take her medicine despite numerous efforts—not to mention, it's not healthy for the cat! I never take it for granted that it will be easy for me to get that pill or liquid down a cat's throat. So make sure your sitter gets a "training run" in your presence before he's left to perform the task on his own.

Beyond pills and liquid mixtures, I strongly recommend that you do NOT expect a cat-sitter to give your cat shots. There are reasons for this that go beyond the basic reality that giving a cat a shot is at least as difficult as popping a pill into Kitty's mouth.

Sticking a pill into a cat's mouth involves some manhandling; you need to be somewhat forceful to get a cat to accept swallowing that nasty little tablet. Sticking a needle into a cat is an order of magnitude worse. It is an act that many cat lovers will have a great deal of difficulty doing, particularly without an extra pair of hands to assist the procedure.

If your cat needs shots of any kind, check with your sitter beforehand to make sure that he has administered shots to a cat before, and that he is willing and able to do so for your cat. This is a situation where having a prior relationship with a sitter becomes invaluable. A sitter who has stayed with your cat multiple times in the past and has already established a rapport with her is the best candidate for being successful at administering shots or pills. Whether your sitter is a longtime friend or a newbie, set up a time when your sitter can come over and go through a trial run on giving your kitty her shot. Only when that happens—and all goes well—can you move forward with your plans to leave that important task in the hands of your sitter.

Under any other circumstances—if your sitter doesn't have experience administering shots, or your cat will not let him give her the shot—I strongly recommend boarding your cat with a vet while you are away. Though that choice will be more expensive in the short run, it will ultimately be best for everyone involved—you, your cat, and the sitter—if a medical professional is allowed to perform this difficult task.

Veterinary Fundamentals

Even if your cat is the picture of health, there are a few cat health care chores that you'll need to check off your task list before you leave.

Make sure you give your sitter the name, address, and contact info (phone number, email, or website) for your cat's regular veterinarian. Let your vet's office know that you'll be away, and that your sitter will be taking care of your cat and is authorized to bring Kitty in if there's a need. Also, if possible, be sure to leave credit card information on file with the vet's office so that your sitter can take your cat to the vet without needing to worry about any payment hassles.

Besides the info for your cat's regular vet, it's also a good idea to leave information on your nearby and preferred emergency veterinary office. The regular vet's info is necessary and helpful, but there's always a chance that an emergency will arise when your vet's office is closed. In that case, your sitter will need an alternate destination to handle any potential off-hours crisis.

Just such a situation happened to me late on a Sunday evening. When one of my clients, Max, fell off a desk and injured his leg, I was very grateful that his human had left the address of a nearby 24-hour emergency clinic that was open and ready to serve.

If you have not looked into the options for an off-hours emergency clinic—many cat companions only have their regular vet in mind—you will be doing both your sitter and yourself a favor by checking your alternate options.

The Ultimate Decision

The vast majority of the time, all will go well for your cat and her sitter. There will, however, be those very rare situations when things will go very, very wrong. It will help everyone involved if you think ahead for just such an occasion, however unpleasant such foresight may be.

My first and most long-standing cat-sitting clients always left instructions that, should either of their cats wind up in an extreme situation, there should be no attempt to keep them alive beyond ordinary measures. I was thankful that the decision would not be left in my hands, and of course I was even more thankful that the situation never arose. Though several of my cat clients left us during my career, none ever went on my watch, much to my relief.

I do want to take this opportunity to stress this to everyone who needs to engage the services of a cat-sitter: if it's at all possible, DO NOT leave it to your sitter to make that ultimate decision. I reiterate the point made at the beginning of this chapter: make sure your cat is in good health before you go away. If your cat is not in good health, if she's sick or old, please consider staying home. If the last moment comes for your cat, she deserves to have you—her best friend—with her at the end. It's hard enough when you have to say goodbye to your own cat; it would be dreadful for a cat-sitter—a person who loves cats—to have to usher another family's cat to the end of her life.

As a cat-sitter, I dreaded the possibility of having one of my cat friends passing away while I was watching them. The best way to avoid that circumstance is for cat companions like yourself to keep your cats healthy, and to stay with them when they're not.

Of course, a cat's health depends upon a lot of factors. One of the biggest influences on whether your Kitty stays healthy or not depends upon whether she is an indoor or outdoor cat. We'll go over both sides of that question in our next chapter.

Chapter 5:
In or Out?

Once upon a time, this chapter's titular question was no question at all. Everyone used to put the cat out at night. Today it's not so simple. Many cat companions live firmly in the "housecat" world. Some cat parents let their kitties outside at least part of the time. Some let their cats out at night, like in the old days; others let their cats out during the day, but bring them in at night. I've even had clients who let some of their cats out some of the time, but kept others in all the time. What's a cat-sitter to do?

One Sitter's Opinion

My personal policy is simple: my family's cats have always been housecats. They don't get to go outside. Period. Whenever one of them went outside, it was cause for quick action—if not outright panic—designed to get her back into the house ASAP. My family has always taken extra care to make sure that our cats stayed safely inside.

When it came to my clients, my feelings were somewhat more mutable. I let my clients' cats out if I was asked to do so. But, as with my own kitties, I preferred then—and still do—that my furry friends stayed inside with me.

Why do I feel this way? Because letting cats outside comes with problems that magnify the worrisome side of caring for someone else's beloved Kitty. It creates a set of challenges that overlay onto the job a whole new dimension of "what can go wrong" anxieties.

The Not-So-Great Outdoors

There are obvious problems with cats going outside. Outdoor cats don't live as long as the ones who stay inside. Cars run over them. Other critters that are a little bigger and meaner than your average pussycat—coyotes spring immediately to mind, raccoons as well—will pick fights with the cats they find out of doors. Those fights often do not end well for the kitties. And some of the two-legged critters out there are not so friendly to cats, either.

As well as finding trouble outside, cats sometimes *cause* trouble out there, too. These days, our felines famously live on trial for the murder—even extermination—of all manner of other species. Kitties can also be blamed for a host of other issues, including messing up other people's property (by using it as a toilet), messing up other people's cats (!), and—perhaps most notoriously—performing their own unique brand of karaoke outside your neighbors' bedroom windows in the dead of night.

The Airlock Principle

Whenever I stayed in a client's home, I got a set of keys so I could get in and out of the place. That's fine and necessary, but if all I got was one key to a front door, that was a potential problem if one of the resident cats was a "door-dasher"—one who is not allowed outside but tries to make her way outside anyway.

Dealing with a door-dasher always adds a layer of stress to cat-sitting. The last thing I ever wanted was to have to chase down an escapee. Once a cat like that gets out, she can be awfully hard to get back in.

That's why, whenever possible, I preferred to enter and exit my clients' homes using the "airlock principle." That is, I always tried to go in and out through some point of ingress and egress that had multiple doors to go through. That way, I could close one door behind me before I opened the second door ahead of me, and there was no way a door-dasher could slip past me and get outside.

The ideal airlock is a garage. If you have a garage and a spare garage door remote to give to

(continues)

your sitter, that's the best plan. Entering and exiting through the garage adds an extra layer of security that helps keep your indoor cat firmly inside.

If your sitter has items to bring into the home—I tend to pack "heavy" when I travel, including when I was on a sitting gig—the garage provides an excellent staging area for transferring stuff from the car to the house. Carrying items in through the front door—even just a grocery bag or two—can give a door-dasher enough time and space to make her hasty exit.

Whenever possible, make sure your sitter has an "airlock" option for getting in and out of your place.

For the record, I grew up in a place—Alameda, California—that has always been a cat haven. Many cats roamed our neighborhood at night, but in all the years I lived there, I experienced the classic "cat wailing in the night" only a handful of times. Cats being noisy neighbors is more myth than fact...though I will admit that it's not completely unheard of.

So there are plenty of reasons why letting a cat outside can mean trouble. In my opinion, it's best to keep them indoors. But some cat companions will not hear of keeping Kitty "imprisoned" within their walls. Thus, out the cat will go.

The Sitter's Dilemma

When you're at home and letting your cat out each day, or night, all is (for the most part) well and good. You let Kitty out, you get to deal with the consequences if something goes wrong.

It's not quite so simple for your cat-sitter. The *raison d'etre* of a cat-sitter is to keep your cat safe and sound (as well as fed and comfortable) while you are gone. Opening that door and letting the cat out fundamentally challenges the cat-sitter's chief goal. Giving a cat access to the not-so-great outdoors entails a certain amount of risk, and because they're dealing with someone else's cats, cat-sitters tend to be risk averse.

How can this dilemma be eased to everyone's satisfaction?

For one thing, make sure you and your sitter understand right up front that the clients (both two-legged and four-legged clients) assume all the risk. The sitter cannot be held responsible for anything that happens to any cat let outside. (I put a disclaimer to this effect on every invoice I presented to my clients. Spelling these things out in black and white beforehand is always a good idea.) As long as these facts are clear to all parties going into the situation, everyone should be able to move forward with relative comfort and security.

Good Outdoor Cat, Bad Outdoor Cat

Even if there's agreement all around that the clients assume the risk for letting the cat go outside, opening that door can still be an unsettling experience for the sitter—particularly if he is, like me, used to not letting cats outside. It took me a while to shake off my discomfort with allowing some of my clients to go outside for the day. Then again, I had other clients who were strictly indoor cats, so I could never completely shake my vigilance against opening that door for Kitty. You'll make things easier for your cat-sitter if you keep a few things in mind when leaving instructions to let the cat out.

Cats who are well-established in their homes—who have lived in their neighborhood for a while and have gone out repeatedly without incident—are the easiest for your sitter to let out without undue worry. This is especially true if you live in a quiet, friendly, non-trafficky neighborhood. Such

Buddy is insistent: "Hey! Let me out already!"

cats are likely to make it back home without much trouble.

The above holds true because cats are territorial. A cat who has been living in your home for a few years has made it part of her territory. Indeed, it's the most important part of your cat's territory—the home base where she gets food, keeps her litter box, and finds comfort, warmth, and safety (not to mention toys and friends). It is the key location in her life, and she won't want to be away from it for too long.

That equation gets tricky if your cat is not so well-established in your home. A relatively new cat may still be in a "trial period" with your home. There's no guarantee that such a short-timer will return to the scene once she strolls out that door.

Things get trickier still if your cats are "troubled" cats: a cat you took in as a stray; a cat who has a history of not liking people; a cat who was abused before you brought her into your home. Then the question of letting the cat outside becomes much more problematic.

Worth a Thousand Meows

These days, with everyone constantly carrying a camera in their pockets via their smartphones, it's hardly necessary to encourage people to take pictures of their cats. But I want to make the recommendation anyway, since having a good, current picture of your cat can be extremely useful, if not actually a lifesaver.

Such a picture becomes vital if your typically stay-at-home house cat suddenly goes rogue and escapes the confines of your home. It happened not too long ago with one of my clients, Audie. A door was accidentally left open, and she sauntered out and disappeared into the night before being missed. The next day, I got an email asking me if I had a recent picture of Audie, to be used for "Lost Cat" flyers. Her human companions didn't have anything other than a snapshot that was about three or four years old, and while Audie had not changed that much in the ensuing years, the photo they had was not the best image of how she looked on the night she made her escape.

(continues)

I was a frequent photographer of my sitting clients, so I was able to supply a photo of Audie that I had taken within the previous year. Fortunately, that photo turned out to be unnecessary; she came back home in good condition after being gone for just one day

It's always good to be prepared; make sure you have at least one up-to-date picture of your cat available for emergencies. A snap from within the last six months should work. You'll be glad you went to the trouble of holding a kitty photo shoot if you find yourself in a searching situation.

Besides, you should be taking pictures of your cats all the time anyway—because they're so pretty, and it's so much fun!

When this stranger you call the cat-sitter arrives and invades the territory, a not-so-well-established or troubled cat may not like that very much. She might just run and hide at first—inside the house if she's already indoors when the invader arrives, or in a well-known and trusted hidey-hole outside if she's already been let out.

If your problematic cat is hiding in the house when her normal time to go outside arrives, that's not necessarily a problem. She might just keep on hiding and not even try to go out when the chance is offered. She'll probably sneak out of hiding during the night, while the sitter is asleep, in order to feed and use the litter, but as likely as not the sitter will wake the next day to find the scaredy-cat right back in that hidey-hole. That's not an ideal situation, but at least there's little risk of anything bad happening to the cat if she chooses to hunker down for the duration.

What happens when your cat-sitter opens the door to the outside world and tells her it's OK to go out? Will she come out of hiding, make a bolt for it, and go? It's hard to say. Different cats react differently. A kitty who has "forted up" might just stay where she is. Cats can have a lot of patience when they want to. A really determined scaredy-cat might very well stay hidden for the cat-sitter's entire visit.

The real crap-shoot begins if and when the scaredy-cat seizes an opening—literally, when the sitter opens the door—and bolts for the outside.

Depending upon just how problematic your cat is, there's a possibility that she might not come back to the house at all. This is especially true if your feeding program involves putting the cat's daily ration out on the patio or some other exterior location. A cat who wants no part of the cat-sitter may just hang around outside and avoid the whole situation entirely. Your sitter could possibly try to "starve" the cat back into the house by not setting out any food, but that would be ill-advised; after all, taking care of the cat is the whole point of the sitting job! Once a problem cat gets outside, the cat-sitter winds up at a decided disadvantage.

Indeed, a troubled and truly determined cat might just say, "Forget this!" and stay outside for the duration of the sitter's stay. I have heard of cats who have stayed out and kept an eye on the house from a distance, watching and waiting for the stranger to disappear and for the acceptable human (you) to return once again.

Finally, there's the really thorny possibility: maybe the cat just disappears and never comes back at all.

When Audie decided to go on an outdoor adventure, it was a good thing I had a recent photo of her!

All of the above applies if you live in a safe neighborhood where there are few external threats to your cat's safety. (Note 'few' and not 'none'; there are *always* some threats to a cat's safety in the great outdoors. Never forget that.) The problem moves into extra dimensions if you live in a heavily-trafficked neighborhood, where there are busy streets and lots of cars; or in an area where there are predators who won't turn up their noses if 'Cat' is on the dinner menu; or in a place where the neighbors are not entirely cat-friendly—even if those neighbors are cats themselves. At the very least, a cat who stays outside for an extended period runs the risk of getting sick or acquiring parasites; fleas might wind up being the least of such a cat's concerns.

Clearly, there's a lot that can go wrong with letting a cat outside—and as a cat-sitter, it's hard not to worry about that.

Unless you've been letting your cats outside for years and years without problems, the safest course to take is to not ask your sitter to let the cat out at all. If you're only going to be gone for a few days, it will not do any lasting damage to briefly deny Kitty her place in the great outdoors. Longer periods will be more problematic, especially for a cat that's used to coming and going (but those cats are the ones who cause the least worry). The bottom line: always err on the side of caution. Let your cat-sitter keep the cat in if it's a viable option, or give him leeway to let the cat out only some of the time. And if your cat fits the "problematic" mold as described above, consider keeping her inside even when you are home.

Hello, You Must Be Going...

Then again, there is another side of the coin. Sometimes, the cat the sitter is watching will make herself a truly unbearable nuisance. Long, yowling serenades (often for no apparent reason), using the sitter as a toy (stealth attacks on the feet and legs are perennial favorites), or picking fights with a feline housemate (the most common troublemaker tactic)—there are any number of ways in which your cat, despite her inherent lovability, might move your sitter towards seeking the sweet relief of escorting the cat outside.

Obviously, if your cat is experienced at taking it outside, then there's no real problem—out she goes, to take her troublesome nature and inflict it on the plants in the garden (or worse). This is a situation where your sitter will want to know if your cat is ever prone to staying out all night; sometimes, it takes that amount of exile to get a naughty cat to turn civilized once more. (I had to employ the after-hours exile on an annoying client a few times in my career. They always came back chastened, either by bedtime or the next morning.)

Then again, sometimes you get this sort of behavior from an indoors-only cat. On this one, your sitter just has to bite the bullet: the cat must stay inside, whatever the behavior. (When the troublesome cat is a loudmouth, a good pair of headphones can be a godsend!) If you ever get any troublemaking behavior with your homebody cat, be sure to mention the most effective remedy to your sitter. For instance, if there's a particular room that serves as the best "detention cell" in the house, be sure to let the sitter know this. A few clicks in "cat jail" can sometimes be the best thing for maintaining household harmony while you're away.

No Changing Beds in Mid-Nap

One final point should be stressed: once you've established whether or not your cat is an outside cat or strictly an indoor cat, don't change that routine without a very good reason.

I know from experience that a cat who has spent the bulk of her life as an indoor cat, who then gets liberty to go outside when she wants, can become a real problem to deal with. Cats, due to their inherently independent nature, are incorrigible liberty-takers; they will take the proverbial mile whenever you offer them an inch. Then, when Kitty doesn't get that mile, she'll act like she's been victimized if her demands are not met.

You may be tempted to change a cat's routine like this because of changing circumstances in the household; for instance, the arrival of a new cat (or two) in the household. (We'll discuss that scenario in greater detail in the next chapter.) I strongly urge you to resist the temptation.

Things don't always work out so well when you make such a change in the middle of a cat's life. A cat who has lived without the experience of going outside may be an easy target for the swarms of trouble that lay in wait out there. Or she just might not be up to the rigors of the outdoor life; there's a reason housecats live longer than the outdoor variety.

Letting cats outside is a recipe for trouble. Keep your indoor cats indoors, and work out whatever issues there are with that lifestyle in some way that's safe, sane, and contained.

As noted, sometimes behavioral troubles arise from the overlap of two cats' territories—namely, your house. There's usually a workable solution to those types of conflict, but often the best solution comes from planning ahead for such situations when you adopt an additional cat in the first place. Our next and last chapter will address a few things to keep in mind when you're thinking about adding a cat to your household.

Chapter 6:
Adding to Your Clowder

A "clowder" is a collective term for a group of cats, like a crash of elephants, or a school of fish, or a murder of crows. I mention "murder" because the question of when it's right to bring a new cat into your home, or how many cats is too many, can be a real killer if you get the answer wrong.

Naturally, the question of how many cats to have in your home is a function of your personal circumstances. It's a matter that lies beyond the scope of anything your cat-sitter will determine. However, my experiences with cats have given me a certain amount of wisdom regarding cat relationships within a home, and there are a few opinions I'd like to share on the subject.

Careful Cat Adopting

As with any major life decision, you will want to carefully consider all the ramifications before you bring a new cat into your home. Before I comment on some of the more nuanced aspects of adopting a cat, let's go over some of the basics for anyone who hasn't yet brought a cat into his or her life.

Where should you get your new friend from? Ultimately, it doesn't matter; if there's a cat that needs a home, and you've got a home that needs a cat—make that match! However, as a longtime volunteer at an animal shelter, I do wish to strongly urge you to get a cat from your nearest shelter. There's nothing a pet store or breeder cat can do for you that a shelter cat can't. You'll get just as much feline love from a "rescued" cat as you will from a pussycat that comes with a hefty price tag.

Should you get your cat from a local, government-run shelter—"the pound" as such places were once called—or should you go to a shelter run by a private organization, the type of dedicated animal welfare facility which has become common in large metro areas? Mostly, that will depend upon what works best for you. The particulars of your situation will decide which facility you visit to get your new cat.

In either case, both the privately-run shelter and the public facility will charge you a certain amount for an adoption fee. Shelter fees will vary by jurisdiction. Cats in most shelters, whether public or private, usually have received veterinary examinations and all necessary treatments, including spaying, neutering and immunizations, before being put up for adoption. The costs of these treatments will be rolled into your adoption fee.

Really, it's that fee that will probably have the most influence upon where you go when you go feline shopping. And because there may be a way to get around paying that fee (or at least most of it), the real question about adopting is not in fact 'Where?' but 'When?'

I learned in my time as a shelter volunteer that adoption fees are not absolute. Since there is always a certain amount of "population pressure" in shelters, both private and public, they are generally motivated to "move the merchandise" so they can open up spots for more cats to come in. That need to keep as many cats as possible moving in and out means that a shelter will, during certain periods, waive part or almost all of a cat's adoption fee to encourage prospective companions to take home a new feline friend. (I say "almost all" because there will still be a small administrative fee to cover costs like keeping the lights on, even if the adoption fee itself has been waived.)

Sometimes fee waivers will happen because the shelter has been given a financial grant that will cover adoption fees for a certain period. Other times, fees will be waived in order to get more cats adopted during a certain period. For example, fees are often waived when "kitten season" is approaching and the shelter wants to have more space available for incoming animals.

However it happens, the best way to take advantage of these "fee free" periods is to plan ahead. When you start thinking about getting a new cat, find your local shelter online (website or social media) and check their latest news posts; they'll probably advertise their fee-free periods there. Find out when the fee waiver period begins and ends, and then start keeping an eye on the shelter's adoptable pets showcase—most shelter websites have a page devoted to pictures and profiles of adoptable animals—to see if anyone strikes your fancy.

Are there any real differences between adoption from a private shelter versus the government-run facility? Does one source have better cats to offer? Maybe, maybe not. A lot of it depends upon where you live and how the local shelters are run.

Both types of shelters tend to have discounted adoption fees at particular times, so financially the decision may be a wash.

As far as 'quality of cats' goes, there may or may not be a difference. I can vouch, from my personal experience, that private shelters tend to be run by people who are very keen on animal welfare, and thus they usually go to great lengths to make sure the animals in their care are healthy and ready to go out the door into a "forever home." The best of the private organizations will weed out the worst "problem cats," meaning any cat that is, for one reason or another, simply not suitable for adoption. Such cats will not make it out onto the adoption floor. So, perhaps, the cat you get from a private shelter is "better" and more prepared to successfully enter your home.

As for government-run shelters, I'm agnostic about them. I confess that I have little experience there; all of my volunteer work was done at a top-notch, privately-run shelter. I have heard from other sources that city or county shelters are sometimes underfunded and understaffed; their priority may simply be maintaining public order rather than tending to full feline welfare. I don't wish to besmirch the work done by anyone who works at "the pound," and I would assume that any cat you get from the local city or county facility will be a fine, healthy and loving cat. My own family's first cat, W.T., came from our city's shelter, and she was a joy to have with us all through her life.

One thing worth noting is that most private shelters are "no kill" facilities, meaning they are committed to keeping their animal guests alive and well until they can find them their "forever homes." If you get your new cat from your local public shelter, there's a pretty good chance you really are saving that kitty's life, while a cat at a private shelter is probably safe until she finds a new home.

Then again, many of the cats who come to the private shelters are actually "rescued" from public facilities, often coming right off "death row" at the government-run shelter. So either way, there's a good chance you'll be saving a life when you adopt your new feline friend; the question may simply be, are you directly or indirectly saving a cat's life when you adopt? Either way, you're doing a good deed—plus you get to have a cat!

Whichever way you go, it is a good idea to stop by your chosen shelter in person a few times and do a little window shopping before you make your choice and adopt a new friend. Just be careful—once you're in there and seeing the kitties face to face, you will be tempted to make an "impulse buy" and take one (or more) home with you that very day.

More Cats Does Not Always Mean More Feline Fun

Whatever road you take to adoption, it's great that you have decided to get a cat. Or I should say, another cat; I assume most of you reading this book are already cat people and have long since shared your home with at least one furry friend. Even so, there are still some important considerations to keep in mind about bringing a new cat into your home, and a few particular circumstances that require some extra thought and care.

As noted above, adopting a cat is mostly about your situation, and all I can do as a veteran cat-sitter is pass along what I've learned about cats leaving and joining households.

In most cases, a cat "leaving" a household means a cat dying. It is a terrible thing when you lose a beloved companion. Most of us in that situation will pause for an appropriate amount of time to grieve for the loss of our dear friend, and only after a certain length of days will we consider bringing a new cat into our homes.

If you have lost your one and only cat companion, the matter is simple: you will want a new cat, and you should go out and get one as soon as you are ready.

However, if you have lost a kitty and have a remaining cat, that's a situation that requires a little more finesse. Bringing a new cat in to live with an established cat—even in situations where there is plenty of living space for multiple cats—can be a very tricky proposition.

Old Cats and New Housemates

Many cats in their natural state are loners. Often, cats spend the majority of their adult lives by themselves—and they generally prefer it that way.

Nevertheless, kitties living in relative harmony with feline housemates is not unknown. Some cats, particularly those that live on farms, have been

Older, established cats like Buster (left) do not always see eye-to-eye with younger newcomers like Lulu.

known to form communities, even sharing tasks such as nursing and guarding kittens. Many cat companions in every variety of home do live successfully with more than one cat in the house—though rarely without at least some level of conflict.

For the most part, I've found that cats are more inclined to tolerate other cats rather than enjoy their company. When you have a well-established cat in your home—one who considers your home to be her territory—bringing a strange cat into that living space may work...or it may be a recipe for disaster.

In my experience, the most quarrelsome cats in one household tend to follow exactly that formula described above: one cat joins a family later than the other. I've seen such situations that have run a whole gamut, from two cats who mostly get along, but occasionally fight with each other, all the way to 'a house divided'—literally divided, where two cats who share a home have to be separated by physical barriers in order to keep the situation tolerable.

If you have a cat and wish to add a second kitty to the household, you need to be prepared for the possibility that things will not go smoothly. A conflict situation is much easier to deal with if you live in a relatively large house where there is plenty of space for multiple cats to keep to themselves. Since separation by physical space is generally the best solution for cats in conflict, it is the one situation where letting cats go outside may be recommended. (Just make sure, as mentioned in chapter 5, that your new cat is fully acclimated to your home before giving her an "escape" option.)

If you are an apartment dweller and have limited space, that's where things get really tricky. There you're talking about a situation where you must Know Your Cat. You need to judge, beforehand, whether or not your current cat has the personality to accept a second cat in the same territory. If there's any negative history between your cat and another kitty—Does she growl at the window if she sees another cat outside? Did she not get along with a prior housemate?—then you may want to consider letting your current cat fly solo for the rest of her time. At the very least, you should be prepared for the possibility that adding another cat into your small living space might turn out to be a very bad idea—one that will only be solved by sending one of the cats into exile. Keeping that potential downside in mind is a must, because once you have adopted a cat and accepted it into your home—and heart—sending it away can be really, really, really hard to do.

Everything that applies to adding one cat to your home applies even more to bringing in multiple new cats. Asking your current kitty to accept two (or even more) new cats into her already established territory has precious little chance of going well for the incumbent cat. The two new cats may get along well together, which will heighten the odds that they will gang up against the more established cat. I strongly recommend against adding more than one cat to your household at a time if there's already a cat living under your roof.

The key thing to keep in mind is that a major change in living arrangements can be enormously stressful for an incumbent cat. Excessive stress, for cats just as with humans, can be a killer. If the cat you already have is a senior cat—for purposes of this discussion, let's say over 10 years old—bringing a new, younger cat into her long-established territory could imperil her health, and maybe even her life.

Remember this fact: cats, when they reach the end of their lives, often falter quickly—a phenomenon referred to as a cat "going down the drain." A cat who seems quite healthy may reach her end suddenly and without much warning. Adding a major stress factor into such a cat's life, like a new housemate, may hasten her downfall in a big way.

So be very cautious about adding cats to your home when there is an already established kitty living there; your current cat's life may depend upon it. If there's any doubt about the current resident's ability to live with other cats, then you probably want to either forgo getting another cat until the incumbent reaches the end of her life, or limit the new arrival to one solitary, non-threatening cat.

That's not to say you will never want to add multiple cats to your home at the same time. When you're in the market to adopt a new cat, you will sometimes find among the available animals a pair of cats who are bonded and (preferably) inseparable. (There will usually be a note to that effect on their shared shelter housing). They may be littermates who have known each other literally their entire lives, or they may just be a pair of cats who have been pushed together by whatever winds of fate govern homeless cats and have taken a liking to one another. However their pair bond came about, such cats can be ideal for bringing maximum feline love into your home at once, especially if you are currently bereft of any kitties. If you're looking to add a couple of cats to your household at the same time, I strongly recommend getting one of those bonded pairs; you will save yourself—and your cats—a world of grief by making sure your cats get along with each other before they ever set a paw in your home.

As noted, sometimes those bonded pairs of cats are kittens who have been together from day one. That makes adopting them in tandem especially appealing; after all, everyone wants a kitten, right?

The Kitten Issue

Kittens can indeed be great. When you adopt a kitten, you don't just get a cat—you get a cat who will spend her entire life with you, and it can be that much easier to form a tight bond with your new baby darling kitty. Plus, given their propensity for play—and habit of finding themselves in goofy situations—kittens are guaranteed barrels of fun. No wonder everyone wants to adopt a kitten.

Kittens may be a popular choice for those looking to adopt a cat, but there are a few things you should keep in mind before you take a kitten home.

When adopting an adult cat, you really want to get a sense of the cat, to make sure you're getting a cat with the right personality for you. With kittens, it's really the other way around: are *you* the right personality for a kitten?

You need to ask yourself a few questions before you adopt a kitten. Am I OK with a boisterous animal running around my home, or do I prefer a quieter household? Am I going to be OK with some of my possessions being broken or ruined by my new cat? (There's a risk of things being broken when you bring any new cat into your home, but it's almost guaranteed when that new cat is still a kitten.) Will you be able to accept it when your rambunctious, fun kitten turns into a mature, calm, adult cat?

Just as a human's personality changes in important ways as they get older, so too can a cat's character shift in various ways. That's not to say that adult cats are necessarily boring—I've rarely

Everyone wants to adopt a kitten like baby Maxi, right?

found them to be so—but they may not be the laugh-a-minute presence in the home that a kitten will be. Be sure that you're someone who won't get bored with your cat after she grows up enough to stop climbing the curtains and jumping up onto the top of the refrigerator.

Of course, if you are someone who prefers a life that's a little "boring," then getting a kitten may not be right for you no matter how much you love cats.

A few years ago, one of my client households adopted a pair of young cats after their senior cat died. The newcomers were not kittens, *per se*; just slightly older than genuine kitten age, something around 6 or 7 months—prime adoption age for bringing a brand-new cat into your life for the long haul.

I sat for them shortly thereafter. One of those cats, Audie (mentioned above; see chapter 5), was friendly, playful, and frisky, but relatively calm for a cat her age. She was easy enough to deal with.

Sometimes, young cats like Puffin go looking for trouble.

But as for Audie's housemate, Puffin? Wow! I couldn't keep up with her to save my life; certainly not my sanity. Puffin didn't just get into trouble; she went on *crime sprees.* She would run from room to room, knocking something over here, making a mess there, moving on to her next work of chaos before I even cleaned up her last bit of ransacking. Puffin made the couple of weeks I spent with her utterly exhausting. I can only imagine what it would have been like to live with her for months at a time before she grew out of her juvenile delinquency. (Puffin did ultimately grow up to be a relatively well-behaved cat, and remains so to this day.)

Before you bring that kitten home, ask yourself the questions listed above. If it turns out that you prefer a more sedate experience in your day-to-day life—meaning, you prefer your stuff to remain in one piece—then you might want to skip the kitten experience and adopt an older cat. You will have plenty of choices in older cats wherever you go to adopt—and you'll still get a cat who will bring you that special kind of feline love that us cat folks have come to adore.

If you feel a kitten will not be right for you, for the reasons listed above, but you still desperately want the experience of playing with a kitten (or two, or four), then I suggest volunteering at your local shelter. Once you get into the shelter's cat socialization program, you will have ample opportunity to spend time interacting with whole litters of kittens—without the danger of any of the belongings in your home being broken. And you can still adopt an older cat to take home with you. It will be like having your kitty cake and eating it, too!

My purpose with this chapter is not to discourage anyone from adopting any cats—far from it! There are so many kitties out there who need homes that any place that has the space—and the desire to share it—should consider getting a cat as soon as possible. But I do want to make sure that you consider all the possibilities that go with bringing a new cat (or two) into your home, so that we can make sure that your adoption experience will be a good one for everyone involved—including the sitter who will eventually be watching those cats for you!

A Special Plea for Some Special Cats

Whenever I talk about adopting cats, I always try to make a special case for black cats and "tuxedo" cats. In my experience, black and black-and-white cats make the best feline friends. The ones I've known have always been among the friendliest, cuddliest, most accepting cats of all my clients. They make great companion cats, and if you're in the market for a new cat, I strongly urge you to consider getting a black or tuxedo cat.

Why are black or tuxedo cats so great? I have a theory.

For a long time, many people, especially in the Western world, disliked cats, and black cats in particular. In their eyes, black cats were viewed with suspicion and superstition. Those unfriendly people were only too willing to kill cats. Whenever those superstitious folks committed their acts of violence against the targets of their hatred, those targets were, as likely as not, the dark-colored kitties among them—particularly those dark-colored cats who had, shall we say, less-than-enchanting personalities.

(continues)

If that notion is true, then the dark-toned cats who survived the persecution were most likely the ones who were protected by kindly people they had befriended due to their more winning personalities. In other words, the black cats with the best natures were the survivors who passed their friendlier genes down to their descendants.

Thus, there was a selection process for black cats with good temperaments. I think that's why today, when you go to adopt a cat at the shelter, many of the sweetest, most loving, and most personable cats in the building will be the black or black-dominant colored cats. Since old prejudices die hard, you will usually find a significant number of black cats on the adoption floor at any given time—meaning there should be at least one ready and waiting whenever you're ready to take a new friend home with you.

So give those black and tuxedo cats a closer look when you're in the market for a new feline friend. You won't regret it.

*Black and white cats like Buster often make
the best feline friends.*

Final Thoughts

I hope this book has enlightened everyone, even longtime cat companions, on some of the most important aspects of living with cats, and about finding the best person to help your feline-loving household when you have to be away.

The last thought I want to leave you with is this: anyone who decides to be a regular cat-sitter is obviously someone who loves cats. When you bring someone into your home to spend time with your cats, he or she will undoubtedly grow to love your cats almost as much as you do. I know that every cat I ever stayed with has, to some extent, "stayed with" me. Even the cats I only spent time with once are still special to me; the cats I cared for over and over again I consider to be some of my best friends in the world. I think of them as "my cats," I love them very much, and I like to think that they love me, too. I hope that you and your cats will also find someone to help them get along while you're gone—someone who will be able to build a relationship with you and your kitties that can grow over the years and enrich the lives of everyone.

Thanks for reading this book, and please give your cats a good scratch behind the ears for me.

Acknowledgments

I wish to thank: Monica Beary and Harvey Wilson, who provided me with my first chance to experience life as a cat-sitter; longtime clients Cynthia Galbraith and Beverly Nikolai, and Jan and Dick Wade, for innumerable visits with their wonderful cats; Mary Heil, for her fantastically beneficial word-of-mouth reference; Sabline Carbaugh for her psychological encouragement and strategic planning assistance; Jacqueline Tootchen, for her editorial assistance with the manuscript; my mom, for being the driving force behind our household becoming cat-friendly; and, of course, all those wonderful pussycats I've had the pleasure to keep company with.

.

CPSIA information can be obtained
at www.ICGtesting.com
Printed in the USA
LVHW080056300921
699099LV00013B/586